Dec. 2016

Unicorn in Captivity

For... To...
" Reg - !
" ! !
Poeter
OVE having you on the East
Coast !

poems by

Marian C. Dornell

Marian C. Dornell

Finishing Line Press
Georgetown, Kentucky

ove e Poetry
Teresa

Unicorn in Captivity

ACKNOWLEDGMENTS

Grateful acknowledgment is due to the editors of the
following journals where these poems (or versions
of them) have previously appeared:

On the Issues: The Progressive Woman's Quarterly:
 "Naomi's Harvest" and
 "Susquehanna Baptism, 1954"

Kinfolks: a journal of black expression:
 "Clarissa Vanishes"

I acknowledge with gratitude lines borrowed from Miriam
Goodman's poem "The Interview," published in her
chapbook, *Expense Report* (Warm Springs Press 1995).

Fledgling Rag, Issue 14, Iris G. Press, 2015:
 "A WPA Writer Interviews a Former Slave"

Editor: Christen Kincaid

Cover Art: Daryl E. Miller

Author Photo: Chuck Fong

Cover Design: Elizabeth Maines

Printed in the USA on acid-free paper.
Order online: www.finishinglinepress.com
                    also available on amazon.com

Author inquiries and mail orders:
Finishing Line Press
P. O. Box 1626
Georgetown, Kentucky 40324
U. S. A.

Table of Contents

I MARIAN

Lessons for a Very Slow Learner.............................1
Come Thursday 2
Colored Neighborhoods.......................................4
A Day at the Lake 5

II NAOMI

Mentee Asee..6
Naomi's Harvest 7
She Weaves 9
Jubilee 11
The Root Woman Reflects on Her Power 12

III UNATTESTED

Antebellum DNA 14
A WPA Writer Interviews a Former Slave 15
Underground..17

IV CLARISSA

Unicorn in Captivity...18
Clarissa Vanishes 20
Elam Breitweist's Susquehanna, 1838 21
Clarissa Speaks, 1839.......................................24

V MARIAN

Susquehanna Baptism, 1954 25
How to Go to a Lynching 26
To Bliss 27
Poem Written in My Mama's Ashes.............................28

For my sister Carolyn Warrick Savage, an avid gardener, whose perennial longing for ancestral stories was the seed for this collection and my brother Scott Warrick, who daily lives the legacy of our ancestors—honor, loyalty, and perseverance

I MARIAN

Lessons for a Very Slow Learner

From the snapshots in the album, it was clear
you didn't have war on your mind when I was born
a month after Germany invaded Poland.
I was two when Hitler and Hirohito
made headlines. You sat by my bed and taught
me the words to "Lift Every Voice and Sing,"
the Negro National Anthem. A few years later
you explained that Rabbi Kern marched
down to city hall so colored children could swim
at the beach by the Susquehanna, while his cousins
were marched into concentration camps in Poland.

That day you smiled and told me *Giuseppe Verdi*
"just meant plain old Joe Green."
I was in third grade and feeling a budding calm.
In the fourth grade, I broke
the promise of a simpler world you tried
to make for me when Mrs. Filmore surveyed
the class on how our fathers earned
a living. The roll moved too quickly.
When it was my turn I said,
"He owns a shoe-shining establishment."
But I was still the daughter of a bootblack.

Come Thursday

Monday morning, home sick from school,
I sat at the kitchen table going over lessons
keeping Mama company. It was her day off.
We listened as "Young Doctor Malone," "Ma Perkins,"
and "Stella Dallas" ducked in and out of troubles.
Jingles jumped over and over again out of the radio
and sang Oxydol bleaching, Rinso whitening,
Super Suds agitating in the growling round
wringer washer with its black-knobbed lid lifted off.

Mama filled the tub with another load of clothes
and more hot water carried in a heavy bucket
from the wood stove. On the back porch, twin
square zinc tubs, filled to the brim, one with bluing
for sheets and Daddy's tee-shirts, the other
with hot starch for cotton dresses with flowers
embroidered on pure white yokes. Daddy always
said the turquoise dress went best with my vanilla
lumpkin's skin. He said in our family he is
a chocolate kiss, Mama a caramel treat.

That woman's Monday hands were tough enough
to dispatch a week's worth of dirt down the drain;
strong enough to lift heavy work clothes from
willow baskets, and steady enough to hang them
on clotheslines that boosted her swaying offering
toward heaven in celebration. Sheets and dresses
clapped hems in praise!

Come Tuesday, that woman could not keep
the teacher from choosing me to be laundress so
white kids could pretend to be ladies and gents. But
on Wednesday someone else had to play laundress
because Mama said I could not be in the play.
Come Thursday, that play was cancelled.

Colored Neighborhoods

The staggered stones in our family plot remind
me of the shacks in the colored part of town,
houses Mama and I have to pass to get
to our hairdresser, who lives
in a neighborhood where the smells
sour the street and I hold my
breath, and the kids threaten to beat me up
when I walk alone to Mrs. Wedlock's.
"Fatback," Mama says. "They cook with
fatback to flavor their pots of greens
and dried beans." "What are greens?" I ask. I grip
Mama's hand tighter because we're walking
a little faster, and it's not getting dark yet.

Hair freshly hotcombed, Mama and I round
the corner to our house of brick
on Liberty Street. We hear the bells
of St. Patrick's Cathedral calling the worshippers
to six o'clock mass. Mr. Duggan,
our neighbor three doors up, climbs
to the top of the steeple three times a day.
Mrs. Bruscia, her lace scarf covering her hair,
scuttles across our street into the churchyard.
She's left some of her fresh pasta sauce
with basil pesto for us on our steps.

A Day at the Lake

Zembo Mosque's dome gleamed bright as the sun;
the swans at Italian Lake swam back-and-forth,
back-and-forth as Daddy peered through his camera lens.
I still hadn't mastered the art of tiptoeing on gravel
and all Daddy-with-his-eyes-in-the-back-of-his-head did
was whisper my name, not in rebuke but in promise
of reprimand if I didn't mind his mantra:
The swans are beauty in disguise. Their wings
are weapons that can hurt if you get too close.
But that didn't sound dangerous enough;
I wanted to steal up to the arched bridge where
my brother skipped stones at the swans, whose wings
spread into a wall of fear, lifting them
from their glassy bed.

II NAOMI

Mentee Asee
Twi people's expression for I don't understand

How will Nyame Dua know it's me who prays to him now?
Didn't Addade bless the fresh altars?

Three moons since slavers attacked our village of weavers;
we wove cloth for our king, stamped

with adrinka pictures. Two moons since my cycle started
with mother too weak to bless me—

I blessed myself. When we finished the long march to the sea,
why did the white men in black robes stand

in front of the boats and motion over our heads as we knelt?
Why did they mutter gutturals

while the boat workers forced the hot irons to our shoulders
closest to our hearts? Human flesh does not

smell like goat flesh at branding time. When I screamed
loud enough to drown out the drums,

did they think it was from pain? Twi people never kneel
before others' gods. The scar

on my shoulder does not hurt anymore. I thought it would
never heal on the long boat ride.

In this place called Philadelphia I trace the scar
of two crossed lines, every day,

in the motion those men in robes made over our heads.
It feels like our symbol for hypocrisy and deceit.

Naomi's Harvest

It's spring
in Fort Hunter, Pennsylvania. The sun
smears magenta, orange, purple over the islands
in the Susquehanna River behind this slave,
a plain stocky woman with black, black skin.
She's dressed in striped wool that sets her apart
from other slaves on the farm, who wear
plain homespun against the chill. Her colors match
the wooly balls she hoards on boards
lining her cabin walls. She is, above all, a weaver.

After trudging part-way up Blue Mountain,
she throws her hoe onto the rocky trail
and wrestles aside the golden bough brush
hiding the clearing she's made for her hush-hush
herb garden. Her Mistress thinks she comes up here
to harvest plant parts for her wool dyes, but
she's already passed those source plants
whose buds have begun to burst—bitter dock,
bouncing bet, bugleweed, tetterwort—scattered
throughout these woods. But on this day she's come
to fetch corms from the stinking Benjamin
whose tea protects her from her nighttime master.

She lifts the hoe to loosen the ground to the rhythm
of her rage. Her corm harvest swells just beneath
the earth. Now, the smell of spring floats up
in big puffs about her boots. The corms sprawl
like veined knuckles. She reaches for one to hold
to her nose, hoping this time she'll finally smell
its stench. But she doesn't. She's never smelled

spring, or anything, in this place. The last smell
she recalls is the odor of her own fear
when the slaver slammed the shovel into her head.

She was twelve then, trying to run after her mother
whose fingers wriggled in rusted cuffs bound
behind her back, the fingers that etched
the shapes of home into her daughter's palms
all the way across the ocean—traced them
to the rhythm of boards creaking over their heads.
She could still smell, then, the human misery
in the belly of the slave ship. Nearly too weak
to speak, her mother traced and retraced
the words of a whispered prayer into Naomi's hands:

Sankofa adinkrahene nyame dua
akoben osrane ne nsoroomma
fihankra sunsum
dame-dame
nyame biribi.

All she recalls of home is in those shapes
she does not know
the meanings of in English.
Still, she hears her mother's voice
and feels the shapes of the words,
somehow retraced in the root tendrils
that cling to the corms.

She packs up her roots, puts on her shawl, hoists
her hoe over her shoulder, and turns to walk back
down the path as the full moon rises over
the darkening ridges on the west side
of the Susquehanna.

She Weaves

for Harry Holder

"Chalang-shooshBANG!" the loom sing-shouts
as Naomi conducts the chorus
of harness, pulleys, pedals, heddles,
sinking sheds, sley hook, cords, and reed.
"Chalang-shoohBANG!" accompanies her thoughts.
They call me slave
but I'm a artist woman, not afraid
of work: I sheared
master's flock before he sold them. I carded
their wool. I'll learn
how to grow
flax, if need be. I grow
the plants that fix the dyes. I boil
the wool. I pull
color from out the air,
color nobody seen. They need me here.
No need for me to run.
I'm sick of folks around here singing
their steal-away songs. Folks who run, they fools.
Master say I'd be the last he sells
because I mean so much to him. He say
I can stay,
even if business keep falling off.
When the money gets better again, he say
he'll start giving me cash for myself. "Soon
as the tavern starts turning a profit again," he say.
""Chalang-shooshBANG!"
Slave catchers came
through again last week. Runaways try to steal
north by way of the Susquehanna. Don't them fools
know ain't no Promised Land on earth?
Ten, twenty years ago we worked forty-strong here:
coopers, carters, teamsters, and wheelwrights,

a miller, planters and harvesters in the fields and gardens,
workers in the stable and smokehouse,
the tavern, mill, hands to keep the springhouse full
of vegetables and fruits from the garden and orchard
and make Master's brandies from his still.
Now, we shriveled to twelve who run this place—
one run away, too many sold.
Master lined us up in the quarters. Gathered us, forced
us to stand outside our cabins. First
come the shuffle-jingle sound of shackled bare feet
coming down the path from the north.
Then you see the parade,
a rickety walking fence.
"Chalang-shooshBANG!"
Them chained together with iron collars
'round they necks. I never seen
the eyes, just they heads hung low, low
as them collars allow.
We thought Master pay them slave catchers
to come through to scare us. They don't have to worry
about me leaving. I free enough.
I free. Enough.
CHALANG-SHOOSHBANG!

Jubilee

Just look at Mistress sitting,
staring out the window. Seems
like she's waiting for her day of jubilee,
same as me.

The Root Woman Reflects on Her Power

Pleurisy root, jewel weed—
they call me the Root Woman.
Hoary puccoon, turtlehead—
got to sort these fine plants quick,
liver leaf and blue-eyed grass.
Master whip me time he knew—
wormwood, cudweed, mugwort, too
—what I'll do with this canoe,
stinkin' sumac, steeplebush.
Susquehanna's gonna be
yarrow and sweet cicely,
soon my ticket to be free.

I coax stillborns back to life,
sit and wait for old folks' death.
I can fix your runny stools
'vacuate your rock-hard bowel.
I can't fix your broken heart,
but I knit your broken bone.
I can stop your nervous twitch,
rid you of your raw red itch.
Make your scalp shed ol' ringworm,
make your seizures quiet down.
Master think he sweet and kind
but he got a treacherous mind.
He makes money off my skill.
I know people, I make pills:
Senecas get dropsy, too,
Tuscarora babes catch the croup;
Amish, they get bad chilblains.

When I run, no more slave pass;
travels will become trespass.
How much freedom I'll have then?
Must find routes to dodge bad men.

III UNATTESTED

Antebellum DNA

It's hard standing here behind Missy
and Teacher, swatting the air to keep
flies away. Wish she could read good
as me so she could move along faster.
Once I almost say *Alabama* for her.
One time Ma'am beat me for telling
Missy the right name for sweet potato:
yam. Aunt Doxie say that's what
they called it back in Africa. Then Mama
give it to me back at the quarters that night.
Seem they don't want nothing African
touching Missy. I can write, too, I think.
I'm too scared to try again. Aunt Doxie near
had a fit time she saw me scratch letters
in the dirt. Made me quick pour water
over my name—turned my name to mud.
She say a slave get her hand cut off
they catch her writing, so I practice letters
in my head. Sometimes I ask Mama to please run.
Then she can buy me. We be free together
someday. Unless I get sold. But she say no.
Seem like Mama like Missy more than me.
Aunt Doxie say me and Missy born the same night.
She say Mama nurse us both that night.
Aunt Doxie birthed us—she say she run back
and forth between Ma'am and Mama the night long,
since Missy and me both had big heads—
nobody in the quarters say why me and Missy
look alike. My hair straighter than hers.
She got blue eyes, too. But I got more freckles.

WPA Writer Interviews a Former Slave
after Miriam Goodman

Where do your people come from?

Wish I knew. Wish I knew where my farthest-back African
come from. When I was a little chap some old man,
older than I am now, he say I'm Ashanti. He say he can tell
where I'm from 'cause I walk like Ashanti and my head
shaped like his people. Say he remember when he was
brought over from Africa. Say the men in his tribe weaved
cloth out of cotton. Some kind of cloth for the king. Then he
say to me, "You and me, we Ashanti. We Ashanti people.
We proud people. Say it! Say Ashanti!" So I say Ashanti.
I say that name every night since because don't nobody
ever talk to me like that before or since. And I been around
—on plantations in Delaware then got sold South 'cause I
tried to escape once—but I always remember what that old
man say. Always remember I come from somewhere else.
Where there's kings.

Did you like your job? What kind of work did you do?

Picked cotton. Hard work. Worked from can to can't. It was
tough work. But that old man say our people grew cotton
so it was like I was feeling something from my homeland
every time I touched it.

What did you do for pleasure?

I liked making shapes in the dirt floor of the cabin. Little
pictures just come to my head. Could never help it. I got
beat lots of times 'cause the driver thought I was writing,
and we wasn't allowed. Reading and writing was against

the law. I tell him I ain't writing, I'm drawing pictures from my head. He made me quit, but the pictures stay in my head to this day. Still don't have no paper or pencil but every night making my supper, I shakes some cornmeal in the pan and make my shapes with my fingers. When I'm through with my shapes, I fix my cornbread.

How do you see your future?

Always wanted to be free. That's my future.

Underground

1. The Quilter

Can't believe the Miss decided
she couldn't do without
my old quilt I put on the fence
as the all-clear signal
for the Railroaders.
Now I got to set up here all hours
to get both Li'l Miss's wedding gown done
and catch up on a new quilt
since there's always runaways.
They say we ain't lost one yet,
and we got more patrollers
in these parts than slugs
roundin' up ripe melons.

2. Lem, Gifted with the Hounds

What they don't know—
how Lem lines their noses
when he hears about an escaped slave
with Mammy Sophie's unguent
so they can't tell shit from a nigger's headrag.

IV CLARISSA

Unicorn in Captivity

Months back when birds was flying North,
Mistress invite her ladies to tea
to tell them about her travels.
She saw big woven pictures, story pieces
of a unicorn, pieces bigger than the bedspreads
Mama Naomi weaves. Mistress say
each picture tells the story of hunters stealing
into the woods to catch a unicorn. The ladies
make sounds out of nature, strange birds trilling
in the woods. When Mistress bring out
her sketches of hunters attacking, capturing,
and killing the unicorn, the room fill up with sound
like a church choir singing Hallelujah at Easter.
Room got quiet when she told how the unicorn
fought those men before they killed it.

Them ladies didn't see me trip
and almost drop the tea tray.
My tears spilled and I wonder why
they so taken with a make-believe animal
stole for pleasure. The ladies wanted to embroider
that unicorn's story, each one make a piece,
six pieces in all. Mistress surprised
me when she said she wanted to teach
me to stitch, to help her with her piece,
"The Unicorn in Captivity," the last piece of the story.

While Mistress taught me how to stitch
the flowers and fruit, she told me
how seed-heavy pomegranates, wild orchids,
thistles, even the tiny frog all stand for marriage
and having babies. Saint Mary's thistle
make your sick stomach better.

Madonna lily and red carnation
mean God's love. Dandelion
was on the table at the Last Supper.
Only thing Mistress didn't say about that unicorn
was why he didn't just jump
that low little fence around him.
I practiced my stitches from her sketches
summerlong. Then Mistress said I learned
enough stitches to fill in the black space
around the unicorn. I know
he's a made-up creature
but he's real to me. When I touch
his shiny white coat, he breathes.
I wonder what he hears. I feel his heart beat slow
like he's at peace. I know
he can't hear what flies over his head—maybe
warblers flying south. When I fly,
I'll fly North.

Clarissa Vanishes

Straw covers Clarissa, pricking
the length of her lying on the floor
of Farmer Breitweist's cart, its sickening
sweet smell nearly distracting
her from the bone-deep pain
from riding over the bumpy path running
along the Susquehanna. The wheels squawk
so that Clarissa thinks this Amish man
needs a good cartwright like Jake
who used to work back at the old place.

She walked away this morning.
Just walked away from the boiling
soap pot, the fire under the cauldron dead
or dying now, the dregs stinking up
the buildings of the place in Fort Hunter:
mill   springhouse   cabins   barn   tavern
even the mansion on the bluff above
the river. Clarissa knows Mistress
is screaming for the boys to run to the spot
on Blue Mountain where she grew the herbs
for her soaps. Scoldings and whippings
she got for staying too long up there
in the early days, but she did not wander
beyond the green birdsong when it was still easy
to climb up the steep brambly slope. Now,
sixty-nine and up for sale, she's counting
on these Railroaders to get her up to Canada.
Is the cart north of the Juniata yet?
She'll need to learn new herbs to grow and to find
folks who'll want the soap that pleased Mistress,
the only thing that pleased Mistress, who
with the family money gone,
said her world was coming to an end.

Elam Breitweist's Susquehanna, 1838

Whoa, Sam, Slim! On a trail following the Susquehanna
just outside Clark's Ferry, Elam eases himself off his seat
and walks stiff-legged to the back of the wagon,

its sheltering coffin filled with other cargo now. He stuffs
two feedbags with the straw that covered his bundles
of wood on the last trip, and drags them to his patient mules.

Over the past decade, not one stick went undelivered
to its destination of the North Branch of this river.
In Lancaster sprawls his lumber yard run by his sons,

and the woodshop where his grandsons apprentice.
Breitweist babies, before hymns from an ancient *Ausbund*
or passages from the Bible, listen to stories

of the family's torture and enslavement in a castle
by the Danube. Three hundred years later,
Elam and his family make fence posts from locust trees,

shape hickory handles for tools, turn fine balustrades
for English mansions in Connecticut. And the coffins.
Always the pine coffins for his bundles of wood.

Yesterday was his last day to tote his cargo upriver
to the North Branch. He leans against a rock, relieved
not to have to listen or be watchful for those other riders

through these woods who hunt for runaways
and those who aid them in defiance of the law. Instead,
he notices the shadbush with its snowy flowers peeking

through the oaks. A pale thing with deep green leaves
creeps toward his boot, catches his eye—one
of Rebecca's healing plants, Trailing Arbutus. She makes

tea when their neighbors get the gravel in their kidneys.
Some call her the best healer in the Susquehanna Valley.
Yes, he decides, taking the empty feedbags back

to the wagon, soon he'll return with Rebecca to this place.
The river peeks through the filigree of leaves. He sees
a blue heron sunning herself and wonders what other birds

will live on these shores when he comes back with Rebecca
which fish will feed along the banks and which loll around
the islands in the middle of the river. He admires the drooping

flowers of Dutchman's Breeches, the delicate white petals
of bloodroot. In Amity Hall, where the Juniata joins
the Susquehanna, he hears horses racing toward him.

The patrollers stop short, their horses' mouths frothing.
Dutchman! You see signs of a old runaway named Clarissa
She come from the McAllister place. Elam's gaze and dumb

response make them suspicious. *What's in that coffin,*
old man? He alights again. At the back of the wagon,
he pries off the lid to expose bundles of hickory branches.

I told you these Dutchmen don't pay no mind to our world.
Leave him be!
There'll be plenty others followin' the North Star.

They ride off, swirling dust around Elam, Sam, and Slim.
Elam secures the coffin lid and takes one last look around.
The next trip north there'll be no time to take in this beauty.

Clarissa Speaks, 1839

I am sixty-nine and finally I get to the Promised Land—
Sand Hill, Nova Scotia.

Land here's fine for growing. I can get my herb garden
started come spring.

Ladies up here on both sides of the color line nice as pie
but they got some nasty skin rashes

on they faces. See If I can't grow some oily plants
to smooth things out—make them pretty

as they think they are. I was twelve when we got sold
off that ship in Philadelphia.

Have mercy, I can still smell the stink—makes my skin
crawl. My first owners' old Auntie Pearl

told me how her people was from a place in Africa
where soap makers mattered, told

about their palm nut gathering, how little ones my age
cracked the nuts open for the oils,

so by age 16 I knew all about soap-making. Then I got
sold to a rich farmer in Fort Hunter, PA.

Seem like soap-making just may be the way to stay free.
See if I can find out how free is free.

V MARIAN

Susquehanna Baptism, 1954

Tucked in a troublesome valley, a brown-skinned girl
sits on her front steps. Above her, the cross
from St. Patrick's blots out the sun. To the east,
the Capitol dome frustrates her vision.
She walks a few streets over to the river,
which flows toward a larger thing, resigned.
It surrenders to the demands of business as usual.
Tugged coal barges skim its shivering skin.
On river's bank this brown-skinned girl
faces the western shore that bars
her kind, where men with anthracite hearts
guard their women and children
from the dark. The brown-skinned girl
scribbles wishes she tosses
into the water, scraps of dreams
drowned like unwanted puppies.
At dusk, debutantes drift by on a flotilla
of party boats, skipping jeweled
stones of light to taunt the brown-skinned girl.
And river flows to a larger thing, resigned.

The girl dives into the water and swims
to an island for a closer look at life
on the far shore. Bridges span
the river, portals that could carry her over,
but she sees a better life than those prisons
of industry with grinning jockeys on their lawns.
So she weaves herself a raft of new dreams
and floats to her own distant shore
moving toward a larger thing, resolved.

How to Go to a Lynching

- get the facts
- "nigger talked back"
- pack a lunch
- drive to the woods
- park your car
- join the crowd
- move in close
- watch me hang
- see me burn
- smell my flesh
- eat your lunch

To Bliss

Now that you know
Your daddy
Hid his blackness
In the shadows
You can't simply slap
On Jemima skin
Like it's suntan lotion
And call yourself
Some ex-white girl from Connecticut
And I can't welcome you to this exclusive
Club with open arms
'Cause we don't have no policy
For when you wanna
Quit.

A Poem Written in My Mama's Ashes

A little colored girl, a nice little colored girl
only simply no more than merely
a nice little colored girl. Mama,
you were the perfect Victorian daughter—
dark doppelganger
of a system that still judges,
labels, estranges, fragments body
from mind
from spirit. You told me, "Be a lady, be a lady,
be a lady in everything you do. Always say "yes, Sir"
and "yes, Ma'am." I asked,
even if they call me nigger with their eyes
while they smile at me?
You said, *this is how you hold your hand*
when you cough and when you sneeze do this;
and always sit with your knees together. Love
thy neighbor as thyself. The meek shall inherit the earth.

I didn't learn until I was older that their hatred
of me was the same as my fear of Jo-Jo, the wild dog
up the street who when he got loose,
chased me because I was more afraid of him
than the other kids were. Mama, you made sure
the Jo-Jo in me never escaped.
Emmet Till's murder hadn't happened yet,
but you knew it was coming.
How could I know those lessons
were for my safety? That those whom I was learning
to fear, feared me more?

You made me practice walking with a book on my head,
and I walked behind you for as many times
it took, from the front room through the dining room
all the way back to the kitchen door and back
to the living room until we could walk five times
without that book falling off my head. Your book never fell.

The first time I tried to escape was the day
I got new skates. Halfway around the block,
my skate came loose,
and I sat on a stone step
to fix it, lifting the heavy steel key from the yarn
around my neck.
I heard a friendly squeak from the door behind me,
and a voice said,
Run along. We don't want colored here.
I locked a moan inside and limp-skated home
after I threw the key away.
I didn't tell you because I didn't want you
to think I'd turned the other cheek
and tried to be like you. I learned your Bible slogans
couldn't make me love a hateful neighbor.

Years later, Mama, I did find some of your footsteps
to follow: I became a nurse, too,
in hospice, Ray's North Carolina inflection
was premeditated seduction. *Why are you
so good to me?* he asked every morning
after I cleaned up his breakfast vomit.

The razor in my gloved hand loitered on the rim
of his Adam's apple. *Why,* I said, *I expect
you'd do the same for me, right?*

His eyes fled mine, and I imagined a door
squeaking open behind me, a voice rasping,
run along. I felt a moan
rise in my throat as I asked myself,
*just why are you being so good to this white
boy?*
Mama, you whispered to me that morning,
Love thy neighbor. The razor retreated.

A retired registered nurse specializing in psychiatric/ mental health nursing and hospice, **Marian Cannon Dornell** lives in Mechanicsburg, PA with her husband, with whom she has five children and six grandchildren. She regularly gives poetry readings in her community as well as talks about race and our society. She has studied with PSU professor and poet Robin Becker and poets Rebecca Foust, Kimiko Hahn, Todd Davis. Her work has appeared in *On the Issues: The Progressive Woman's Quarterly, Kinfolks: a journal of black expression,* and won an honorable mention in the 2013 Concrete Wolf Chapbook Contest.